Baby & Toddler
Meal Planner

Baby & Toddler
Meal Planner

igloo

Published in 2012
by Igloo Books Ltd
Cottage Farm,
Sywell,
NN6 0BJ.
www.igloo-books.com

0312 C005

2 4 6 8 10 9 7 5 3 1

ISBN: 978 0 85780 504 1

Food photography: Clive Bozzard-Hill
Picture acknowledgements: GETTY IMAGES 7, 8, 13, 15, 31, 37
JUPITER 22, 25, 53, 77 MIKE HEMSLEY/WG PHOTO 2, 11, 18

Printed in China

Contents

Food and your child

A love of food is one of the best gifts that you can give your child. By introducing your baby to homecooked food from the start, you can lay the foundations of healthy eating – something that will stand him or her in good stead for life.

Many people turn to commercial baby foods for convenience. However, there are plenty of quick, nutritious meals that you can make from fresh ingredients. Giving your baby homecooked food allows you to introduce a much greater variety of taste and texture than is possible with bought baby foods. It also means that you know exactly what he or she is eating.

All the recipes in this book are easy to do, and none take long to prepare. Most make several meals at a time, so that you can freeze them in small portions, and then defrost and heat them when needed. There are ideas for every stage of the weaning process, from first vegetable purees to meals that the whole family can share.

Relaxed eating

Your child is more likely to develop a good attitude towards food if you make mealtimes happy, social occasions. Sit and eat with your baby when you can, and include your children in family meals as often as possible. It's natural for a baby to want to explore the texture and feel of food, so be relaxed about mess – put a plastic sheet on the floor, put a plastic bib on your baby, and enjoy the fun he or she gets out of mealtime.

All parents want their children to eat a good diet, but it is important that food does not become a source of conflict. If you try to force your child to eat vegetables, for example, then he or she will learn that refusing them is a good way of getting your attention. Far better, to remove the untouched food without comment and then to offer the same vegetable at a later date. Similarly, don't take refusals too seriously. Children have likes and dislikes, but they often need to be offered a food over and again – maybe as many as 10 times – before they will try it. They may also take a sudden dislike to a food, then happily devour it the next day.

In the end, healthy eating is a habit your child should enjoy learning. Don't worry if he or she doesn't eat everything you offer. So long as you serve a range of foods, your baby will almost certainly get the nourishment he or she needs.

Guide to the recipes

The quantities for each recipe are given in both metric and imperial measures. They are not exact conversions, so you should stick to one system rather than mixing them. Every recipe in this book is coded with symbols to let you know at a glance how long it takes to make, whether you can freeze it, and how to serve it.

You can freeze this dish.

How long it takes to prepare and cook the dish, from start to finish.

Serve the dish warm.

Serve the dish cold.

When to introduce solids

Signs that your baby is ready for solid food:

- Your baby is about six months old.

- Your baby can sit up well with support.

- Your baby is genuinely interested in food, and may try to grab it out of your hand.

- Your baby can pick up food in the fingers and bring it to the mouth.

- Your baby wants to chew *(and may have teeth)*.

- Your baby seems hungry after a feed, or wants more frequent feeds *(this could also be due to a growth spurt, so increase milk intake first)*.

When to Start

All babies are different, but six months is usually the ideal time to start introducing solid food. At this age, a baby's iron stores begin to run out, and he or she will almost certainly be ready for first foods. A six-month-old baby also has the physical skills necessary for eating: he or she can usually sit upright (with support) and has lost the tongue-thrust reflex that pushes things out of the mouth. Most importantly, a baby's digestion will be mature enough to handle most foods.

Until recently parents were advised to start weaning their babies at four – or even three – months. However, we now know that breast milk or infant formula provides all the nutrients that babies need for the first six months. Starting solids very early or giving certain foods before the age of six months can trigger infections or allergies (see page 12).

Some babies take to solids more quickly than others. If your baby doesn't show much interest in food, then you may want to wait a little longer before starting him or her on solids. Premature babies are often ready for solid foods later than full-term ones. Consult your health provider if you are unsure about when to start solids.

Food and sleep

Parents often want to give their baby solid food because they think this will help him or her to sleep through. However, studies have shown that starting solids does not improve a baby's sleep. Generally speaking, it is an increase in brain activity – not hunger – that makes an older baby prone to waking up at night; he or she needs to learn good sleep habits. In any case, extra milk feeds are usually the best way to deal with any increase in hunger before six months.

Essential equipment

You can hold your baby on your lap for his or her first tastes of food. But sooner or later, you will probably find that it is more convenient to put your baby into a high chair. Consider using one that you can pull up to the table, so that your baby can join in family meals from the start. To wean your baby, you will probably also need:

- two or three shallow bowls (so that your baby can see what he or she is eating).

- two or three small, shallow weaning spoons.

- three or four bibs (waterproof ones that cover the arms as well as the body).

How to start

The key to introducing solids is to take it slowly. At first, your baby is just experimenting with the idea of food, and with new tastes. Your baby is still getting the calories and nutrients he or she needs from milk. Breast milk and infant formula contain more nutrients than the equivalent amount of baby rice or fruit or vegetable puree. There are different ways to introduce your baby to solid food. Most people like to start with smooth purees before introducing mashed food and finger foods, and then gradually build up to family food chopped small enough for the baby to manage. Don't give a baby smooth purees for too long, or he or she may refuse lumpier foods.

If you have waited until your baby is six months to start solids, you do not have to give purees at all. Instead you can give food that is well mashed, and you can also give some finger foods from the start. Many babies prefer to feed themselves rather than be fed from a spoon.

The first feed

You should give your baby food when he or she is calm, but not sleepy. Mid-morning is often a good moment. You can offer food on a clean fingertip or a spoon, or by placing it on a feeding tray for your baby to pick up.

If using a spoon, don't try to push it into the baby's mouth – a baby that is interested in food will open his or her mouth, and may even lunge towards the spoon. If your baby shows little interest in the food, don't try to make him or her take it. Let your baby decide when and what to eat. Always stay close by when your baby is eating in case of choking.

Your baby's milk

Milk will remain the major part of your baby's diet even after solids have been introduced. You will probably find that your baby takes varying amounts of milk from day to day.

If you are breastfeeding, continue to feed on demand. If using formula, your baby needs at least 500-600 ml/about 1 pint a day until the age of one. There is no need to switch from infant formula to follow-on milk unless you feel that your baby needs it – talk to your health adviser if you are unsure. Cow's milk is not suitable as your baby's main drink until at least one year, but small amounts can be used in cooking.

What food?

Start with simple foods, including finger foods for babies of
six months and over. These could include:

- Baby rice, mixed with your baby's usual milk.

- No-salt rice cakes.

- Purees of steamed root vegetables.

- Steamed vegetables left whole or cut into sticks *(such as
  green beans or carrot sticks)*.

- Purees of stewed fruits such as apple or pear.

- Ripe fruits such as banana or papaya, well mashed.

- Finger-shaped pieces of ripe banana, slices of ripe pear or
  papaya, or thin slices of steamed apple or pear.

Feeding your baby

Start with one 'meal' a day. Your baby will probably take only tiny amounts of food at first, and you can gradually increase the amount as your baby's appetite grows. Build up to two, then three or four meals a day.

As your baby gets more familiar with eating, you can give a greater range of foods. Babies often enjoy strong tastes, so don't assume that your child won't like, say, cheese, plain (natural) yogurt, or spinach. Herbs and mild spices are a good way of making your baby's food taste more exciting – try sprinkling a little cinnamon on morning porridge, for example.

A healthy diet

Once your baby is eating two or three meals a day, you can begin to balance his or her diet by incorporating a good mix of foods. Offer each of the following foods each day:

- Fruits and vegetables, which are good sources of fibre and vitamins. Serve yellow, orange, red, and green vegetables to get a range of nutrients; dark leafy vegetables contain iron and folic acid.

- Cereals, such as rice, oat porridge, and pasta. These foods contain energy-rich carbohydrate. However, don't let your child fill up on carbs at the expense of other nutritious foods.

Foods that are known to be allergenic should not be given to any baby before the age of six months. These foods include:

- Wheat products and other foods with gluten.
- Milk (do not give as a drink before 12 months).
- Eggs (do not give egg white before 12 months).
- Soya products.
- Fish and shellfish (do not give shellfish before 12 months).
- Peanuts, nuts, and seeds (see also page 15).
- Citrus fruits, berries, kiwifruit, and tomatoes.

Start your baby on simple foods **(see page 11).**

When your baby is established on solids, introduce allergenic foods one at a time, leaving three days between each new food in case of a reaction. If you or your partner have a history of allergies – including asthma, eczema, or hay fever – then your child is more at risk of developing allergies. Exclusive breastfeeding for the first six months is the best way to protect your baby. You may want to wait until your child is one year before giving allergenic foods, and should wait until he or she is three before giving peanuts. See your health carer for specific advice.

- Meat, chicken, fish, eggs, and pulses. These foods are high in protein, which is needed for growth. If your child is vegetarian, give two servings of protein foods a day. Vegan diets are not recommended for young children.

- Dairy products. These contain calcium, which is needed for strong bones and teeth. If your child cuts down on milk, serve twice a day.

Drinks

Offer your baby sips of water at mealtimes (though this is not necessary if you are breastfeeding on demand). Give water in a cup, and use tap water rather than bottled mineral water, which is not suitable for babies. There is no need to boil water for your baby to drink provided that he or she is over six months.

Fruit juice contains fructose (natural sugar), which can cause tooth decay. It is best given to older children only. If you do give juice to a baby over six months, give it only at mealtimes and dilute it well: one part juice to ten parts water.

Fizzy drinks, squashes, and teas should not be given to young children.

Cooking for your baby

Homemade food made from fresh ingredients usually tastes much better than commercial baby foods, and it is a lot healthier for your child than processed foods.

Steaming is one of the best ways of cooking fruits and vegetables because it preserves most of their nutrients. Boiling, baking (without oil), and broiling (grilling) are also healthy cooking methods. Foods that are fried or roasted can be hard for babies to digest so they should be avoided until the child is one year old, and then given only sparingly. Microwaving is very quick, but it destroys some of the nutrients in food. It also heats unevenly so you should not use a microwave to warm a baby's milk.

Batch cooking

It is a good idea to cook a batch of baby meals in one go, freezing several portions in ice-cube trays or small containers. This will save you from cooking meals from fresh every time. Transfer the cubes to a freezer bag once they are frozen, remembering to date and label the bag.

You can defrost most baby foods by warming them in a pan with a little water to prevent them from sticking. Some dishes such as those containing fish are best defrosted in the refrigerator first. Take care to heat the food through thoroughly, then let it cool before serving to your baby.

Food safety guidelines

Babies are more susceptible to stomach upsets than adults, so you need to take extra care to prepare their food safely.

- Always wash your hands before preparing food or feeding your baby.

- Prepare food on a clean surface.

- Do not prepare your baby's food if you are vomiting or have diarrhea.

- Wash fruits and vegetables well.

- Clean all feeding equipment thoroughly.

- Wash your baby's hands before each meal, and after it, too.

- Keep prepared food in the refrigerator until your baby is ready to eat it.

- Always heat food thoroughly, then let it cool before serving it to your baby.

- Throw away leftover food in your baby's bowl – saliva from your baby's spoon will introduce bacteria which will then multiply.

- Keep uncooked meat and fish away from your baby's food.

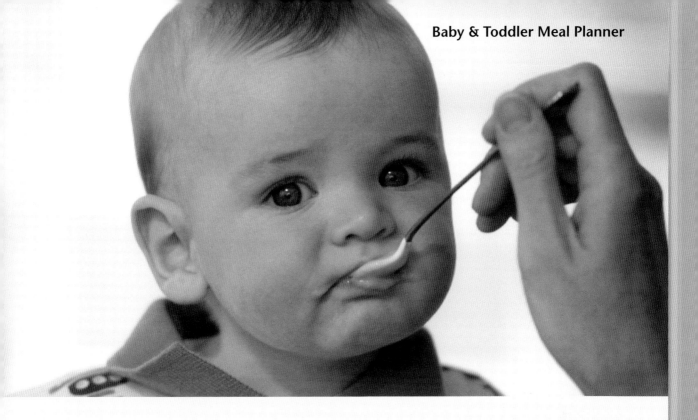

Foods to avoid

Babies over six months can eat most foods, but the following should be avoided.

- **Salt.** A baby's immature kidneys cannot process salt well, so do not give salty foods or add salt when you are cooking. Choose low-salt bread, unsalted butter, and unsalted rice cakes.

- **Sugar.** Sugary foods fill your baby up without providing nutritional value. Avoid giving cakes, biscuits, and sweets for as long as you can. Homemade cakes and biscuits are usually better for your child than store-bought ones.

- **Honey.** Do not give honey to a baby under 12 months (honey occasionally contains a bacterium that causes infant botulism).

- **Whole or crushed nuts.** Nuts are a choking risk. Do not give whole nuts to a child under five. Smooth nut butters are a good way of giving protein-rich nuts to a baby over six months, so long as there is no risk of allergy.

- **Low-fat foods.** Young children need high-energy foods, so always give full-fat dairy products rather than low-fat ones. Children over two years can switch to low-fat dairy products providing they are eating well.

- **High-fibre foods.** Brown rice, bran, and other high-fibre foods fill a baby up without providing sufficient nutrients. Stick to white rice and white pasta for young children.

What food when:
at-a-glance guide to feeding your baby

	0–6 months	6 months	7 months	8 months
MILK	Breast milk is a perfectly balanced food containing all the nutrients a baby needs. Infant formula is the best alternative food for the first six months.	Milk is still your baby's most important food. Continue breastfeeding on demand, or offer formula (500–600 ml/ about 1 pint a day).	Give sips of water at mealtimes. Get your baby used to drinking from a cup rather than a bottle.	
FRUIT AND VEGETABLES		Introduce cooked apple and pear, raw ripe pear, banana, papaya, or avocado. Other first foods include cooked squash, carrot, sweet potato and potato.	Introduce more cooked orraw, ripe fruits: melon, nectarine, plums, apricots.Introduce more cooked vegetables: zucchini (courgette), parsnip, broccoli, green beans, spinach, cauliflower.	Incorporate garlic, herbs, or mild spices to make food taste more interesting.
CEREALS		Offer gluten-free baby rice mixed with your baby's usual milk, or well-mashed cooked rice. Unsalted rice cakes can also be given.	Introduce other grains: porridge oats, millet, corn, quinoa, wheat. Give white rice, bread, and pasta rather than brown.	Toast fingers and breadsticks make good finger foods.
MEAT, FISH, EGGS, AND OTHER PROTEIN SOURCES			Chicken and lamb are the most easily digested protein foods to give.	Introduce other meats, fish (but not shellfish), pulses, and well-cooked egg yolk (but not egg white).
DAIRY PRODUCTS			Introduce plain (natural) yogurt, pasteurized cheese, and small quantities of cooked cow's milk with food.	
HOW TO SERVE YOUR BABY'S FOOD		Offer small amounts of food – 1–2 tsp/5–10 ml – every day. You can give mashed foods and some soft finger foods as well as smooth purees.	Gradually offer more food, keeping pace with your baby's appetite. Give food two to three times a day, preferably when you or others are eating.	

9 months	10 months	11 months	12 months	1 year +
	Your baby will probably drop a milk feed once he or she is eating several meals a day.			Breastfeeding continues to have benefits. Many women feed for two years or longer. Toddlers should have at least 350 ml/12 fl oz of milk a day.
		Serve fruits and vegetables as snacks and as part of most meals.		Aim to give at least five servings a day. Avoid offering juice until your child asks for it, then dilute well and limit to one cup a day, to be drunk at mealtimes.
		Serve every day, but with other foods rather than on their own.		
Nuts can be given in the form of a smooth butter. Do not give if your baby is at risk of allergies.		Serve protein foods every day. If your baby eats no meat, give two servings of alternatives a day.		Whole eggs can be given, but they should still be well cooked. Shellfish can be given. Do not give whole nuts to children under five because of risk of choking.
		Serve every day if your baby has reduced his or her milk feeds. Offer full-fat rather than low-fat versions.		Full-fat cow's milk can be given as a drink (offer it in a cup rather than in a bottle).
Give finely chopped, ground (minced), or grated foods as well as healthy finger foods.		Most babies can manage foods that are chewy or lumpy. Some foods may need to be finely chopped.	Offer three or four meals a day, plus healthy snacks such as fruit between meals.	Include your baby in family meals wherever possible.

First stage planner (6 months)

Introduce first foods one at a time, so that you can see how your baby responds to each new taste – he or she may show real enjoyment in pear, say, but reject banana. Remember that your baby is experimenting with the idea of eating at this stage; he or she gets most of the necessary nutrients from milk. It doesn't matter when you give your baby food, but choose a time when he or she is neither sleepy nor very hungry.

The first week

Here is a suggested first week of solid foods to try. But feel free to substitute other first foods if you prefer.

Day 1	Baby rice mixed with your baby's usual milk
Day 2	Baby rice mixed with your baby's usual milk
Day 3	Carrot puree or steamed carrot sticks
Day 4	Baby rice mixed with your baby's usual milk
Day 5	Pear puree or thin slices of steamed pear
Day 6	Baby rice mixed with your baby's usual milk
Day 7	Carrot puree or steamed carrot sticks

First tastes meal planner

Once your baby has tried a few single fruits and vegetables, you can start combining them to introduce him or her to more complex tastes. Here is a second week of foods to try.

Day 1	Creamy vegetable puree
Day 2	Parsnip and apple puree, or slices of steamed apple
Day 3	Parsnip, carrot, and rutabaga (swede) puree
Day 4	Pear and apple puree, or slices of steamed pear
Day 5	Butternut squash and zucchini (courgette) puree
Day 6	Banana and papaya puree, or slices of these fruits
Day 7	Green bean puree, or steamed whole green beans

Second stage planner (7-9 months)

Once your baby is used to first tastes, start to widen his or her repertoire. Give at least some foods with soft lumps, even if your baby has no teeth; he or she will use the gums to chew. Introduce finger foods if you haven't already done so; give easy-to-hold foods that are soft or dissolve once sucked (for example, rice cakes or steamed carrot sticks). You may like to give a sweeter fruit dish after a meal, but don't feel you have to give a dessert every day. Build up to two meals a day, but remember that your baby still needs as much milk as before.

	BREAKFAST	LUNCH	DESSERT
Day 1	Baby rice with apple puree	Chicken, carrot, and green bean puree	
Day 2	Rice cakes with mashed banana	Vegetable soup, toast fingers	Berry dessert
Day 3	Baby rice with pear puree	First fish pie	
Day 4	Oat porridge, peeled slices of ripe nectarine	Broccoli and sweet potato puree	Slices of steamed apple
Day 5	Baby rice with mashed papaya	Curry & rice	
Day 6	Baby rice with pear puree	Three veg cheesy mash	Melon puree, or a half-slice of melon
Day 7	Toast fingers with mashed banana	Creamy vegetable puree with added spinach puree	
Day 8	Oat porridge with apple puree	Chicken, carrot, and green bean puree	Slices of ripe papaya
Day 9	Baby rice with melon puree	Toast fingers with mashed avocado	
Day 10	Natural (plain) yogurt with mashed banana	First fish pie	Berry dessert
Day 11	Rice cakes with mashed or peeled slices of ripe papaya	Parsnip and apple puree	
Day 12	Oat porridge with apple puree and a tiny pinch of cinnamon	Curry & rice	Peeled slices of very ripe pear
Day 13	Baby rice with nectarine puree	Vegetable soup with toast fingers	
Day 14	Toast fingers with mashed banana	Three veg cheesy mash	Plain (natural) yogurt

9-12 months meal planner

Gradually build up to three meals a day, plus healthy snacks. Young children often need to eat earlier than grown-ups: as well as breakfast, try lunch at 11.30 am and supper at 5 pm. If you are breastfeeding, continue to feed on demand. If bottle-feeding, continue with infant formula or follow-on milk. You may find that your baby drops a feed, but he or she should still be having at least 500–600 ml/1 pint a day.

Snack box

Small children tend to eat little and often. Here are some healthy snacks to enjoy between meals:

Dried fruit: raisins, apricots, pear, apple rings, papaya, mango *(give dried fruit no more than once a day).*

Grain foods: rice cakes, sugar-free rusks, toast fingers, slices of pita bread or chapati.

Mini sandwiches, with sliced or grated cheese, homemade houmous, or smooth nut butter *(unless there is a risk of allergy).*

Vegetables: Cooled cooked carrot sticks, whole green beans, or bell-pepper strips, sliced raw tomato, sliced cucumber.

Fresh fruit: slices of pears, banana *(cut into 'sticks')*, nectarine, melon, and papaya, tangerine segments *(any pips removed)*, quartered grapes *(whole ones are a choking hazard).*

	BREAKFAST	LUNCH	SUPPER
DAY 1	Oat porridge with pear puree	Three veg cheesy mash Slices of melon	Lamb stew with rice
DAY 2	Yogurt, nectarine slices, toast	Pea risotto Fruit compote with yogurt	Pita pockets with home-made houmous, cooled steamed carrot sticks, and green beans
DAY 3	Wheat biscuit cereal with papaya slices	Tomato pasta sauce Raspberries and quartered, seeded grapes	Chicken casserole
DAY 4	Oat porridge with banana and cinnamon	Curry & rice and green beans Berry dessert	Macaroni cheese and broccoli
DAY 5	Fruit compote, yogurt, toast fingers	Couscous salad Ripe pear slices	Lamb stew with baby pasta shapes
DAY 6	Wheat biscuit cereal, quartered grapes	Fish plov with broccoli Plain yogurt with mango slices	Ratatouille with mashed potatoes
DAY 7	Rice cakes, mashed banana	Vegetable soup, toast fingers Baby fruit salad	First fish pie
DAY 8	Oat porridge with cinnamon and raisins	Pea risotto	First fish pie and steamed carrot sticks
DAY 9	Wheat biscuit cereal, quartered grapes	Pita pockets with homemade houmous, cucumber sticks Pear slices and raisins	Macaroni cheese with broccoli
DAY 10	Oat porridge with apple puree	Mini sandwiches with cream cheese and grated carrot Banana	Chicken casserole
DAY 11	Toast fingers, sliced pear	Curry & rice with chopped spinach stirred in Berry dessert	Vegetable soup, baby pasta shapes
DAY 12	Toast, yogurt, melon slices	Couscous salad Papaya slices	Fish plov with steamed green beans and carrots
DAY 13	Oat porridge with mashed banana	Lamb stew with rice Fruit compote	Tomato pasta sauce
DAY 14	Toast fingers, slices of papaya	Ratatouille with rice Baby fruit salad	Curry & rice

Toddler meal planner

By the age of one year, most children will be eating at least three meals a day with healthy snacks. Milk remains an important food – your toddler still needs at least 350 ml/12 fl oz a day. Your child can eat most of the same foods as you (with some exceptions and modifications), and it is a good idea to eat together whenever possible. Here is a suggested two-week menu that incorporates both toddler meals and family meals for you all to enjoy.

	BREAKFAST	LUNCH	SUPPER
DAY 1	Oat porridge with mashed banana	Watercress soup with bread and butter	Lemon chicken with rice towers, steamed green beans Baby fruit salad
DAY 2	Low-salt, low-sugar cornflakes, apple slices	Mini sandwiches with tasty spread, cheese chunks, carrot sticks, and cucumber slices Strawberries with yogurt	Spicy rice with chicken
DAY 3	Wheat biscuit cereal, nectarine slices	Hot fish triangles Berry dessert	Ratatouille with rice and broccoli
DAY 4	French toast, quartered grapes, half a banana	Egg strips with soupy noodles and sugarsnap peas	Baked beans with baked potato and cheese Slices of mango
DAY 5	Oat porridge with yogurt, sliced pear	Pita pockets with homemade houmous, cucumber sticks, and tomato slicesFruit compote with yogurt	Pasta with pepper pasta sauce, broccoli
DAY 6	Everyday pancakes with fruit puree	Mini cheese sandwiches, with carrot and celery sticks Easy-cook cookie with fresh blueberries	Shepherd's pie with peas
DAY 7	Low-salt, low-sugar cornflakes, half a banana	Chicken nuggets with rice and sugarsnap peas	Borshch with garlic bread Hot raisin apple
DAY 8	Oat porridge with pear puree and cinnamon	Pasta bolognese with peas Raspberries with plain (natural) yogurt	Pea risotto
DAY 9	Wheat biscuit cereal, nectarine slices	Macaroni cheese with broccoli Orange muffin	Winter sausage hotpot with steamed green beans
DAY 10	French toast, tangerine	Potato cake with tomato slices and cucumber sticks Cheese star, raisins	Mini fishcakes with peas and runner beans
DAY 11	Toast, yogurt, apple or pear slices	Lamb stew with three-veg cheesy mash Berry dessert	Speedy pizza with cucumber sticks and tomato slices
DAY 12	Low-salt, low-sugar cornflakes, slices of papaya	Mushroom carbonara	Fish plov with steamed green beans Baby fruit salad
DAY 13	Everyday pancakes with fruit puree	Couscous salad Banana, dried apricots	Chicken casserole
DAY 14	Oat porridge with pear puree	Tomato pasta sauce Easy-cook cookie and strawberries	Curry & rice, sugarsnap peas

First stage foods

Here is a selection of first dishes to give your baby. They include purees of root vegetables and simple fruits (apples, pears, banana, and papaya), and baby rice – all foods that are easy to digest. Once your baby has had his or her first tastes, you can combine different purees for greater variety and introduce stronger-tasting fruits and vegetables.

Baby rice

Unlike most other cereals, rice contains no gluten, so it is an excellent first food for babies. It's easy to make your own baby rice, but be sure to use white rice rather than brown, which is hard to digest.

Makes **6** Baby Portions

$^1/_4$ cup/50 g/2 oz basmati rice

$^1/_3$ cup/75 ml/3 fl oz cooking water or your baby's usual milk

1. Wash the rice well under running water. Fill a small pan with water, bring to a boil, then add the rice. Stir once, cover, then simmer over low heat for 15 minutes, until the grains are very soft.

2. Drain, reserving $^1/_3$ cup/75 ml/3 fl oz of the cooking water, if using. Add the milk or the reserved cooking water, and blend or mash.

Carrot puree

Carrots have the sweet taste that babies naturally prefer, and they are a good source of beta carotene, the plant form of Vitamin A.

Makes **4** Baby Portions

2 medium carrots, peeled and cut into slices (leave organic carrots unpeeled)

splash of the cooking water or your baby's usual milk

1. Place the sliced carrot in a steamer, and cook over a pan of boiling water for 15 minutes, until very tender. Alternatively, simmer in a little water for 10 minutes.

2. Blend or mash the carrots, adding a little of the cooking water or your baby's usual milk to get the desired consistency.

Butternut squash puree

Another beautifully sweet vegetable that babies seem to love. Squash is easily digested and so makes an ideal weaning food. You can use ordinary squash or pumpkin instead if you prefer.

Makes **8** Baby Portions

1 small butternut squash, peeled, seeded, and cut into
   small chunks

splash of the cooking water or your baby's usual milk

1. Place the chopped squash in a steamer and cook over a pan of boiling water for 10 minutes, until very tender.

2. Blend or mash the cooked squash, adding a little of the cooking water or your baby's usual milk to get the desired consistency.

Pear puree

Pears are very easy on a baby's stomach and are often recommended as the first weaning food. If your baby is over six months and the pear is very ripe, you can simply mash it without cooking.

Makes **6** Baby Portions

2 pears, peeled, cored, and cut into slices

splash of the cooking water or your baby's usual milk

1. Place the sliced pears in a steamer and cook over a pan of boiling water for 7–8 minutes, until very soft. Alternatively, place in a pan with 3 tbsp/ 45 ml water and simmer for 5–6 minutes.

2. Blend or mash, adding a little of either the cooking water or your baby's usual milk to get the desired consistency.

Apple puree

Apple, like pear, makes a versatile puree – serve on its own, with baby rice, or, later on, stirred into your baby's morning porridge. Choose a naturally sweet eating variety rather than a baking (cooking) apple.

Makes **4** Baby Portions

1 eating apple, peeled, cored, and cut into slices

splash of the cooking water or your baby's usual milk

1. Place the sliced apple in a steamer and cook over simmering water for 8–10 minutes, until very soft. Alternatively, place in a pan with 3 tbsp/ 45 ml water and simmer for 7–8 minutes.

2. Blend or mash, adding a little of either the cooking water or your baby's usual milk to get the desired consistency.

Creamy vegetable puree

This simple puree combines baby rice, milk, and sweet root vegetables. For a stronger taste, try adding a spoonful of spinach or broccoli puree to it.

Makes **6** Baby Portions

1 medium carrot, peeled and sliced
   (leave organic carrots unpeeled)

1 slice butternut squash, peeled, seeded, and cut into
   small chunks

3 tbsp/45 ml baby rice (see page 26)

1. Place the sliced carrot and the chopped squash in a steamer and cook over simmering water for 15 minutes, until very soft.

2. Blend or mash, adding a little of the cooking water to get the desired consistency, then combine with the baby rice for a creamy puree.

Creamy fruit puree

A combination of first fruits and baby rice. This dish makes a quick breakfast cereal that will remain popular long after your baby has graduated to more grown-up foods.

Makes **10** Baby Portions

1 eating apple, peeled, cored, and cut into slices

1 pear, peeled, cored, and cut into slices

3 tbsp/45 ml baby rice (see page 26)

1. Place the sliced apple and pear in a steamer and cook over simmering water for about 10 minutes, until very soft.

2. Blend or mash, adding a little of the cooking water if needed. Combine with the baby rice.

Sweet potato puree

Sweet potato tastes good whether it is steamed, boiled or oven cooked.

Makes **4** Baby Portions

1 yellow-fleshed sweet potato, scrubbed

splash of your baby's usual milk

1. Preheat the oven to 200°C/400°F/Gas Mark 6. Prick the skin of the sweet potato with a fork, then cook in the oven for 40 minutes, until soft. Halve lengthwise, spoon out the flesh, and mash with the milk.

2. Alternatively, peel the sweet potato and cut into small chunks. Cook in a steamer over simmering water for 25 minutes, or place in a pan, cover with water, bring to a boil, then cook for 15 minutes. Mash with the milk or a little of the cooking water.

Potato puree

Potatoes are a good source of energy, and they also provide vitamin C and fibre. Their mild taste works well with sweet root vegetables, and also with spinach and broccoli.

Makes **8** Baby Portions

1 large starchy (floury) potato, scrubbed

splash of your baby's usual milk

1. Preheat the oven to 200°C/400°F/Gas Mark 6. Prick the potato skin with a fork, then cook in the oven for 1 hour or until soft. Halve, spoon out the flesh, and mash with your baby's usual milk.

2. Alternatively, peel and cube the potato. Steam for 25 minutes, or cover with water, bring to a boil, and cook for 20 minutes, until soft. Mash well, adding a little of the cooking water or your baby's usual milk to get the desired consistency.

Rutabaga (swede) puree

Rutabaga (swede) is a good source of vitamin C. Like most root vegetables, it has a naturally sweet taste that babies enjoy. Try combining it with parsnip and carrot for a tasty three-veg puree.

Makes **5** Baby Portions

$^1/_2$ rutabaga (swede), peeled and cut into small chunks

splash of the cooking water or your baby's usual milk

1. Place the rutabaga (swede) in a pan of boiling water, reduce the heat, and simmer for 15 minutes, or until very tender.

2. Blend or mash, adding a little of the cooking water or milk to get the desired consistency.

Parsnip puree

Choose young, small parsnips which are sweeter than the older, woody ones. This vegetable is a useful source of fibre, as well as vitamins C and E. It goes brilliantly with apple.

Makes **4** Baby Portions

2 small parsnips, peeled

splash of the cooking water or your baby's usual milk

1. Cut the woody core from each parsnip, and then chop into small chunks. Place in a pan of boiling water, reduce the heat, and simmer for 20–25 minutes, until very soft.

2. Blend or mash, adding a little of either the cooking water or your baby's usual milk to get the desired consistency.

Zucchini (courgette) puree

Zucchini (courgette) is good on its own or combined with potato, sweet potato, or butternut squash. Do not peel this vegetable as most of the nutrients are in the skin.

Makes **4** Baby Portions

1 medium zucchini (courgette), trimmed and cut into slices

splash of the cooking water or your baby's usual milk

1. Put the zucchini (courgette) slices into a steamer and cook over simmering water for 10–12 minutes, until very soft

2. Blend or mash to a soft puree, adding a little of the cooking water or your baby's usual milk to get the desired consistency.

Broccoli puree

Once your baby is well established on solids, serve green vegetables on a daily basis so that your child gets into the habit of eating them. Most babies love broccoli, and it is packed with nutrients.

Makes **5** Baby Portions

$1/2$ head of broccoli, cut into small florets (discard the thick part of the stalk)

splash of the cooking water or your baby's usual milk

1. Place the florets in a steamer and cook over simmering water for 10–12 minutes, until very tender. Blend or mash, adding a little of the cooking water or your baby's usual milk to get the desired consistency.

2. Alternatively, once your baby is having finger foods, steam the florets for 5–6 minutes, until cooked, and serve whole.

Green bean puree

Use French beans rather than runner beans which tend to be rather stringy. This puree is good mixed with baby rice, potatoes, or sweet root vegetables. You can use steamed green beans as a finger food from six months.

Makes **1** Baby Portions

6 green beans, topped and tailed

splash of the cooking water or your baby's usual milk

1. Place the beans in a steamer and cook over simmering water for 10–12 minutes, until very soft. Alternatively, cook in boiling water for 8–9 minutes.

2. Blend to a puree, adding a little of either the cooking water or your baby's usual milk to get the desired consistency.

Spinach puree

Introduce nutritious spinach early enough, and your child will take to it as readily as to any other food. It is best combined with another vegetable: carrot, sweet potato, or rutabaga (swede) work well.

Makes **5** Baby Portions

225 g/8 oz baby spinach leaves

splash of the cooking water or your baby's usual milk

1. Wash the spinach well, then place in a pan with 2 tbsp/30 ml water. Cover the pan and cook over low heat for 3–4 minutes, until well wilted.

2. Blend with a little of the cooking water or your baby's usual milk to get the desired consistency.

Banana puree

Bananas are every parent's standby. They taste beautifully mild and they are one of the few foods that younger babies can eat uncooked. Bananas are a good source of the mineral potassium.

Makes **2** Baby Portions

1 small banana

splash of your baby's usual milk (optional)

1. Cut the required amount of banana, leaving the rest in its skin (it will keep for a day in a cool place). Remove the skin, then mash until smooth, adding a little of your baby's usual milk if needed.

2. Once you have introduced finger foods, cut a third of a banana into 4 lengthwise slices and place on your baby's feeding tray for him or her to pick up.

Papaya puree

Papaya is another instant puree. Like banana, it mashes well. Try it on its own or mixed with banana or avocado.

Makes **1** Baby Portions

1 slice of papaya

splash of your baby's usual milk (optional)

1. Remove the seeds from the papaya slice. Take off the skin, then use a fork to mash the flesh to a smooth consistency, adding a little of your baby's usual milk if needed.

2. Once you have introduced finger foods, cut a slice of papaya in half crosswise, remove the seeds, and wash the rind well. Place on your baby's feeding tray for him or her to pick up.

Melon puree

Ripe melon is a wonderful no-cook food suitable for babies over six months. Cantaloupe melon is the most nutritious variety and it has the sweetest taste.

Makes **1** Baby Portion

1 slice of melon

1. Remove the seeds from the melon slice. Take off the skin and mash with a fork until smooth.

2. Once your baby is having finger foods, give him or her half a slice to chew on (remove the seeds and wash the rind first).

Nectarine puree

Ripe nectarine or peach can be eaten raw once your baby is well-established on solid foods (and so long as he or she is over six months). Make sure the fruit is very soft and ripe.

Makes **4** Baby Portions

1 small nectarine or peach

1. Cut the fruit into quarters, twisting to detach it from the stone. Pull the skin off each quarter, starting at the stalk end. Mash the flesh to a smooth consistency with a fork.

2. Once your baby is taking finger foods, offer a thin, peeled slice of nectarine for him or her to try.

Second stage foods

Once your baby gets used to the idea of eating, start giving a wider variety of food. Here are some great-tasting ways to introduce protein-packed foods such as chicken and cheese.

All these dishes are suitable for babies over six months and your baby can enjoy finger foods, too – try simple homemade bread rusks, rice cakes, slices of soft ripe fruit, and steamed vegetables served whole or cut into sticks.

Three veg cheesy mash

Most babies love the consistency of mashed potatoes, and this version gives them a range of vegetables in one easily digestible package. You could use parsnip or carrot instead of the rutabaga (swede).

Makes **12** Baby Portions

2 large starchy (floury) potatoes, peeled and diced

1/2 small rutabaga (swede), peeled and diced

1 small sweet potato, peeled and diced

splash of your baby's usual milk

1 tbsp/15 ml olive oil

1/2 cup/50 g/2 oz grated Cheddar or other hard cheese

1. Place the potatoes, rutabaga (swede), and sweet potato in a pan and cover with cold water. Bring to a boil, and cook for 20 minutes or until very soft.

2. Drain the vegetables, and add the milk and oil. Mash until smooth. Then add the grated cheese and stir to mix.

Chicken, carrot and green bean puree

This simple recipe is a good way of introducing protein-rich chicken to your baby's diet. Chicken has a mild taste that goes well with most vegetables.

Makes **8** Baby Portions

1 small chicken breast, skin left on

1 tsp/5 ml olive oil

1 large carrot, peeled and diced
   (leave organic carrots unpeeled)

50g/2 oz fine green beans, topped and tailed

splash of your baby's usual milk

1. Preheat the oven to 180°C/350°F/Gas Mark 4. Place the chicken breast on a lightly greased baking sheet. Brush with the oil and cook in the oven for 20 minutes or until cooked through.

2. Meanwhile, steam the carrots for 10 minutes. Add the green beans to the steamer, and cook for 5 minutes longer or until the vegetables are soft.

3. Remove the skin from the cooked chicken and discard. Cut the flesh into small chunks. Place in a blender with the cooked vegetables and the milk. Blend to the desired consistency.

Homemade rusks

Teething babies like to have something hard to chew on, but most teething biscuits contain sugar. These simple bread rusks are easy to make and have a pleasingly crunchy texture. Older kids often enjoy them as well.

Makes **24** rusks

$^1/_2$ loaf good-quality unsliced bread

1. Preheat the oven to 140°C/275°F/Gas Mark 1. Cut the bread into slices 1 cm/$^1/_2$ in thick, then cut off the crusts and discard. Cut the slices into fingers about 1 cm/$^1/_2$ in wide.

2. Place the bread fingers on a baking sheet. Cook in the oven for 40 minutes, or until they are crisp all the way through. Let cool before serving, and keep in an airtight box for up to a week.

Vegetable soup

A classic leek and potato soup with carrots for added sweetness. This recipe appeals to babies, toddlers, and grown-ups alike. You can stir in some chopped parsley if cooking for adults.

Makes **20** Baby Portions

1 tbsp/15 ml olive oil

4 large starchy (floury) potatoes, peeled and cut into chunks

2 medium leeks, sliced

2 medium carrots, peeled and sliced
   (leave organic carrots unpeeled)

5 cups/1.2 l/2 pints hot vegetable stock
   (use homemade or a good, low-salt bought stock)

natural (plain) yogurt, to serve

1. Heat the oil in a pan over medium-to-high heat. Add the potatoes, leeks, and carrots. Cook, stirring, for 5–6 minutes, until the vegetables are starting to brown and soften.

2. Add the stock and bring to a boil. Turn down the heat, cover the pan, and simmer for 25–30 minutes or until the vegetables are very soft. Blend to a smooth consistency. Serve on its own, or with a dollop of yogurt stirred in (do not add yogurt if you are planning to freeze the soup).

Curry & rice

Lentils are a good non-meat source of protein to give your baby. This mild curry combines lentil dhal with rice and yogurt for a balanced all-in-one dish that freezes well.

Makes **10** Baby Portions

$^1/_2$ cup/100 g/$3^1/_2$ oz red lentils, well rinsed

$^1/_2$ garlic clove, peeled and sliced lengthwise slice of peeled ginger root

1 bay leaf

1 cup/200 g/7 oz basmati rice

2 tbsp/30 ml natural (plain) yogurt, to serve

1. Place the lentils in a pan. Cover with water (the water should be 1.5 times the depth of the lentils). Bring to a boil, skimming off any 'froth' that appears on the surface of the water. Add the garlic, ginger, and bay leaf, then reduce the heat, cover the pan, and simmer for 40 minutes, or until the lentils are soft and soupy.

2. Meanwhile, cook the rice in a pan of boiling water for 10 minutes, or until tender. Drain, reserving the cooking water. Use a fork to mash the rice, adding as much of the cooking water as needed. Alternatively, leave the grains whole.

3. Remove the ginger, garlic, and bay leaf from the lentils, and discard. Add the cooked rice and stir to combine. Serve with the yogurt stirred in (do not add yogurt if you want to freeze the dish).

First fish pie

Fish is fantastically good for you: it is high in protein and full of nutrients. Introduce it from about 8 months. If you are freezing this dish, be sure to defrost and then reheat it thoroughly before serving.

Makes **10** Baby Portions

2 large starchy (floury) potatoes, peeled and cut into equal-
   sized chunks

175 g/6 oz skinless white fish fillet

full-fat milk, enough to cover the fish

knob of butter

1 tbsp/15 ml olive oil

freshly grated nutmeg, to season

1. Put the potatoes into a pan of cold water, bring to a boil, then cook for 20 minutes or until tender.

2. Meanwhile, place the fish in a small pan, and pour in enough milk just to cover the fish. Bring to a boil, then take the pan off the heat, and let the fish cook in the hot milk. When the fish is opaque and cooked through, remove from the milk, and carefully flake, discarding any bones. Strain the milk and reserve.

3. Drain the potatoes and mash with the butter, olive oil, a little grated nutmeg, and 4 tbsp/60 ml of the reserved milk. Combine with the flaked fish, and serve.

Berry dessert

This healthy dessert, suitable from about 8 months, may tempt a reluctant eater. Cottage cheese is appealingly creamy, with an interesting texture that will help your baby get used to food with lumps.

Makes **1** Baby Portion

$^1/_4$ cup/25 g/1 oz cottage cheese

berry fruit puree

$^1/_4$ cup/25 g/1 oz frozen or fresh berries such as raspberries, blackberries, redcurrants, or blackcurrants

1 tbsp/15 ml water

1. Make the fruit puree. Place the berries in a small pan with the water. Cook over medium heat for 4–6 minutes, until the berries disintegrate. Let cool completely, then press through a strainer (sieve) to make a smooth sauce.

2. Spoon the berry sauce over a cone-shaped mound of cottage cheese.

Food for 9-12 months

By now your baby will probably be familiar with a good range of foods, which means that you can give him or her a varied and interesting diet.

These recipes include foods that you can take out with you, as well as baby-friendly meals to enjoy at home. It's a good idea to get your child eating proper meals at this stage, so that he or she can progress to sharing family food.

Pea risotto

Risotto is a wonderful introduction to more grown-up food – and it is a meal that all the family can share. This is a classic pea risotto with optional mushrooms for extra taste.

Makes **10** Baby Portions / Serves **4**

2 tbsp/30 ml olive oil

1 medium onion, finely chopped

1^1/$_2$ cups/280 g/10 oz Arborio (risotto) rice, rinsed

3^1/$_4$ cups/700 ml/1^1/$_4$ pints hot vegetable stock
  (use homemade or a good, low-salt bought stock)

knob of butter

175 g/6 oz flat mushrooms, finely diced (optional)

^{2}/$_3$ cup/85 g/3 oz frozen peas

1. Heat the oil in a thick-bottomed pan, add the onion, and cook for 7–8 minutes, until softened but not browned. Add the rice and then stir for 1–2 minutes to coat thoroughly in the oil.

2. Add the stock a ladleful at a time, stirring constantly, and waiting until the liquid is almost absorbed before adding more. Continue stirring until all the stock has been used and the grains are tender – this will take about 20 minutes.

3. Meanwhile, put the butter into a small pan and melt over medium heat. Add the mushrooms and reduce the heat to low. Cook for 6–7 minutes, until thoroughly cooked.

4. When the rice is cooked, stir in the peas, and cook for 5 minutes until heated through. Add the hot mushrooms and their cooking liquid just before serving.

Lamb stew

Lamb is a great weaning food: it is very digestible, and as a red meat it is an excellent source of iron. This stew is made with ground (minced) lamb which is easy to chew. Serve with rice or baby pasta.

Makes **12** Baby Portions

1 tbsp/15 ml vegetable oil

450 g/1 lb lean ground (minced) lamb

1 large onion, peeled and finely chopped

2 large carrots, peeled and diced
   (leave organic carrots unpeeled)

2 medium zucchini (courgettes), diced

225 g/8 oz mushrooms, chopped

1¼ cups/300 ml/½ pint hot vegetable stock
   (use homemade or a good bought low-salt stock)

400 g/14 oz can chopped tomatoes

1 tbsp/15 ml tomato puree

pinch of dried mixed herbs

2 tsp/10 ml cornstarch (cornflour)

¼ cup/50 ml/2 fl oz water

1. Preheat the oven to 180°C/350°F/Gas Mark 4. Heat the oil in a flameproof, ovenproof, lidded casserole. Add the ground (minced) lamb in 2 batches and brown over high heat – each batch will take 3–4 minutes. Remove from the pan with a slotted spoon and set aside.

2. Reduce the heat to low, add the onion and carrot to the oil in the casserole, and cook for 6–7 minutes, until softened. Add the browned lamb together with the zucchini (courgettes), mushrooms, hot stock, tomatoes, tomato puree, and herbs. Stir, bring to a boil, then cover and place in the preheated oven for 40 minutes.

3. Remove the stew from the oven, and use a spoon to skim any excess fat from the surface. Combine the cornstarch (cornflour) with the water. Add to the casserole, and bring to a boil before serving.

Tomato pasta sauce

A delicious tomato sauce that offers a surreptitious way of upping your child's veggie intake. If you want a very smooth sauce to use as a pizza topping, omit the carrot and zucchini (courgette), and blend well.

Makes **10** Baby Portions / Serves **4**

1 tbsp/15 ml olive oil

1 small onion, chopped

1 garlic clove, peeled and crushed

1 zucchini (courgette), grated

1 medium carrot, peeled and grated
   (leave organic carrots unpeeled)

400 g/14 oz can chopped tomatoes

squeeze of tomato puree

large pinch of dried mixed herbs

1 bay leaf

freshly cooked small pasta shapes, to serve

1. Heat the oil in a saucepan over low heat. Add the onion, garlic, zucchini (courgette), and carrot. Cook gently for 6–7 minutes until soft, but do not allow the vegetables to brown.

2. Add the tomatoes, tomato puree, mixed herbs, and bay leaf. Stir well. Bring to a boil, then turn the heat down low, cover the pan, and simmer for 30 minutes or until thickened. Stir occasionally.

3. Remove the bay leaf, then blend the sauce until smooth (you can leave it lumpy if you prefer). Stir a spoonful of the sauce into the cooked small pasta shapes, and serve.

Pita pockets with houmous

Houmous is perfect picnic food, so it's worth introducing in the first year when your baby is open to new tastes. It contains tahini, a sesame-seed product, so is not suitable for young babies or children at risk of allergies.

Makes **20** Baby Portions / Serves **4**

400 g/14 oz can chickpeas

2 garlic cloves, peeled and crushed

juice of 1 lemon

3 tbsp/45 ml olive oil

$^1/_3$ cup/50 g/2 oz tahini

pinch of cayenne pepper

mini pita pockets, to serve

few alfalfa sprouts or curly cress (optional)

cucumber sticks, to serve

1. Put the chickpeas into a blender with the garlic, lemon juice, oil, tahini, and cayenne. Blend to a thick paste the consistency of peanut butter.

2. Lightly toast the mini pita pockets. Cut them in half and let cool.

3. Spread a little houmous inside each pita half. Add the alfalfa sprouts or cress, if using. Serve with cucumber sticks alongside.

Macaroni cheese with broccoli

An all-in-one meal that's ready in minutes. Only the sauce is suitable for freezing – be sure to defrost it before cooking and then heat very slowly with a splash of extra milk to stop it sticking to the pan.

Makes **6** Baby Portions / Serves **2**

1¹/2 cups/175 g/6 oz small macaroni

broccoli florets, to serve

cheese sauce

¹/2 stick/50 g/2 oz butter

1 rounded tbsp/15 g/¹/2 oz all-purpose (plain) flour

1¹/4 cups/300 ml/¹/2 pint full-fat milk

¹/2 tsp English mustard

  (or ¹/3 tsp mustard powder mixed with 1 tsp water)

pinch of cayenne pepper

1¹/2 cups/150 g/5¹/2 oz grated strong Cheddar cheese

1. Cook the pasta in a large pan of boiling water until softened but still firm to the bite. At the same time, steam the broccoli for 8–10 minutes, until tender.

2. Meanwhile, make the cheese sauce. Place the butter in a small pan over low heat, and melt. Stir in the flour, and cook for 2–3 minutes, stirring all the time. Add the milk very slowly, continuing to stir as you do so (it may go into a single lump at first, but keep on stirring). Bring the mixture to a boil and immediately take the pan off the heat. Add the mustard and cayenne pepper, stirring well, then stir in the grated cheese.

3. Drain the pasta, and cover with the sauce. Slice the tree-shaped broccoli florets into manageable pieces, and serve with the macaroni cheese.

Couscous salad

This simple dish is a useful alternative to sandwiches if you want food to take out and about. A small pot of plain yogurt and a banana or ripe pear would make good accompaniments.

Makes **2** Baby Portions

$^1/_4$ cup/25 g/1 oz couscous

$^1/_3$ cup/75 ml/2$^1/_2$ fl oz boiling water

1 tsp/5 ml olive oil

$^1/_4$ cup/25 g/1 oz frozen peas

1 small tomato

2.5 cm/1 in piece cucumber, cut into small dice

15 g/$^1/_2$ oz Cheddar or other hard cheese, cut into small dice or grated

1. Place the couscous in a cup or small bowl, and pour the boiling water over the top. Stir in the oil, cover, then leave for 3–4 minutes until the grains plump up.

2. Meanwhile, cook the peas in a pan of boiling water, then drain and add to the couscous.

3. While the peas are cooking, put the tomato into a cup, pour some boiling water over the top, and wait for 1 minute. Cut into quarters, then pull off the skin. Chop the flesh into small dice. Add to the couscous and pea mixture with the cucumber and cheese. Stir to combine.

Fish plov

Plov is a Central Asian rice dish – it's known as pilaf or pilau elsewhere.
If you want to freeze this, make it with salmon rather than white fish,
which does not freeze as well.

Makes **12** Portions / Serves **4**

1¹/₄ cups /225 g/8 oz basmati rice

280 g/10 oz salmon fillet or boneless white fish fillet

knob of butter

2 tbsp/30 ml olive oil

1 medium onion, chopped

2 garlic cloves, crushed

¹/₂ cup/50 g/2 oz frozen peas

small handful of fresh parsley, finely chopped

freshly ground black pepper, to season

1. Preheat the oven to 180°C/350°F/Gas Mark 4. Cook the rice in a pan of boiling water for 10 minutes or until tender. Drain and set aside.

2. Place the fish on a sheet of foil. Dot with the butter, then enclose the fish in the foil to make a loose parcel. Put onto a baking sheet and cook in the preheated oven for 15 minutes, until opaque and cooked through.

3. Meanwhile, heat the oil in a thick-bottomed non-stick pan, add the onion and garlic, and cook for 7–8 minutes until soft. Add the cooked rice and the peas, then cook for 5 minutes longer.

4. Flake the cooked fish carefully, removing any bones. Add the fish, any buttery juices, and the parsley to the rice mixture. Season, and cook for a further 2–3 minutes to heat through.

Ratatouille

A tasty vegetarian dish that works equally well served with mashed potatoes, pasta or rice. Try grating some cheese on top or stir in a spoonful of natural (plain) yogurt before serving. Older children like this just as much as babies.

Makes **10** Baby Portions

2–3 tbsp/30–45 ml olive oil

1 small onion, finely chopped

1 red bell pepper, seeded and finely diced

1 small eggplant (aubergine), finely diced

2 medium zucchini (courgettes), finely diced

2 large mushrooms, diced

4 large tomatoes, skinned, seeded, and chopped

squeeze of sundried tomato paste

small handful of fresh parsley, finely chopped

1. Put the oil into a pan, and place over medium heat. Add the onion, bell pepper, eggplant (aubergine), zucchini (courgettes), and mushrooms, and cook for about 15 minutes until the vegetables are soft.

2. Add the tomatoes, tomato paste, and parsley. Stir, then cook for 15 minutes longer, until everything is cooked. Add a splash of water if necessary to prevent the vegetables from sticking.

Chicken casserole

This chicken casserole has a delicious herby taste. Everything is cut into baby-sized pieces so that it is easy to eat. Serve with green beans alongside.

Makes **16** Baby Portions

3 tbsp/45 ml vegetable oil

2 large skinless chicken breasts, chopped into small dice

2 leeks, sliced lengthwise into quarters and then chopped finely

450 g/1 lb new potatoes, left unpeeled and chopped into
   small dice

2 cups/450 ml/16 fl oz hot chicken stock, or enough to cover
   the chicken and vegetables (use homemade or a good,
   low-salt bought stock)

handful of fresh parsley or tarragon, finely chopped

large pinch of dried mixed herbs

freshly ground black pepper, to season

450 g/1 lb large flat mushrooms, finely chopped

2 tsp/10 ml cornstarch (cornflour)

$1/4$ cup/50 ml/2 fl oz water

1. Heat 2 tbsp/30 ml of the oil in a large, heavy-bottomed pan. Add the diced chicken in 2 or 3 batches, and brown over high heat – each batch will take 2–3 minutes. Set aside.

2. Add the remaining oil to the casserole, add the leeks and potatoes, and cook for 6–7 minutes, until they begin to brown. Return the browned chicken to the pan with the vegetables, then add the hot stock, the herbs, and the seasoning. Bring to a boil, then reduce the heat, and cover the pan.

3. Simmer for 15 minutes, or until the potatoes are cooked, stirring occasionally. Add the mushrooms and cook for another 5–6 minutes, until cooked.

4. To thicken the sauce, add the cornstarch (cornflour) to the water, then stir to dissolve. Stir into the chicken casserole, then bring back to a boil before serving.

Fruity compote

This simple, vitamin-packed compote will keep for two to three days in the refrigerator. It's lovely with porridge, or you can serve with Greek or natural (plain) yogurt for a delicious dessert.

Makes **4** Baby Portions

5 ready-to-eat dried apricots, chopped

2 ripe pears, peeled and chopped

1 large nectarine, stoned, peeled, and chopped

2 tbsp/30 ml apple juice

2 tbsp/30 ml water

2.5 cm/1 in piece of cinnamon stick

Greek or natural (plain) yogurt, to serve (optional)

1. Place the apricots, pears, and nectarine in a small pan with the apple juice and water. Add the cinnamon stick.

2. Bring to a boil, then turn down the heat, cover the pan, and simmer for 8–10 minutes, until the fruits are very soft.

3. Remove the cinnamon stick. Let the compote cool before serving with the yogurt, if using.

Baby fruit salad

A selection of fresh fruit chopped into tiny pieces is about as healthy a dessert as you can get. This one uses papaya, mango, and nectarine, but you could substitute sliced melon, lychees, and quartered grapes if you liked.

Makes **2** Baby Portions

$^1/_4$ papaya, peeled and stoned

$^1/_4$ mango, peeled and stoned

$^1/_2$ nectarine, peeled and stoned

juice of 1 orange

Greek or natural (plain) yogurt, to serve (optional)

1. Chop the fruit into small, manageable dice and place in a bowl.

2. Pour the freshly squeezed orange juice over the top and stir to mix. Set aside for 15–30 minutes to allow the tastes to meld. Serve the fruit salad on its own, or with yogurt.

Food for toddlers

With the exception of salty, very spicy, or highly processed foods, toddlers will happily eat many of the same things as adults. So now you can have meals together more easily. All these recipes are tried and tested on young children. Many of them appeal to adults too, making them great choices for family meals. There are also some healthy treats for you and your children to make together.

Watercress soup

This green-flecked soup contains watercress which is rich in vitamins and minerals – it's one of the healthiest fresh salad vegetables you can get. The soup makes a lovely family lunch, served with bread and cheese.

Makes **12** Toddler Portions / Serves **4**

2 tbsp/30 ml olive oil

2 small leeks, cut lengthwise and sliced

750 g/1 lb 10 oz starchy (floury) potatoes, peeled and cut into equal-sized chunks

4 stalks of celery, sliced

5 cups/1.2 l/2 pints hot chicken or vegetable stock (use homemade or a good, low-salt bought stock)

1/2 tsp/2.5 ml freshly grated nutmeg

freshly ground black pepper, to season

handful of fresh parsley, chopped

100 g/3 1/2 oz watercress, thick stalks removed

1. Heat the oil in a large pan, then add the leeks, potatoes, and celery. Cook over low heat for 10 minutes, stirring from time to time, until the vegetables are slightly softened.

2. Add the hot stock with the nutmeg and black pepper. Bring to a boil, then reduce the heat, and let simmer for 30 minutes, until all the vegetables are tender.

3. Add the parsley and the watercress, and cook for 1 minute longer. Blend until smooth.

Pepper sauce for pasta

This robust, fresh sauce will appeal to grown-ups as well as toddlers.

Serve with green vegetables such as sugarsnap peas, green beans or broccoli.

Makes **10** Toddler Portions / Serves **4**

1 tbsp/15 ml olive oil

1 medium onion, chopped

1 garlic clove, peeled and finely chopped

1 red bell pepper, seeded and cut into thin strips

1 yellow bell pepper, seeded and cut into thin strips

400 g/14 oz can chopped tomatoes

1 tbsp/15 ml sundried tomato paste

small handful of fresh basil, chopped

freshly ground black pepper, to season

freshly cooked pasta shapes, to serve

grated Cheddar or Parmesan cheese, to serve

1. Heat the oil in a thick-bottomed pan. Add the onion, garlic, and bell peppers, then cook over low heat for 15 minutes, or until softened, stirring from time to time.

2. Add the tomatoes to the pepper mixture with the tomato paste, the basil, and the pepper. Increase the heat to medium, and cook for a further 20 minutes, until slightly thickened.

3. Serve over freshly cooked pasta shapes, with a sprinkling of grated Cheddar or Parmesan cheese on top.

Herby garlic bread

Garlic bread is almost universally popular, and it is a great way of getting kids used to strong tastes early on. Serve this crusty treat on its own as a snack, or with a bowl of homemade soup.

Makes **12** Toddler Portions

1 day-old baguette

2 garlic cloves, peeled and crushed

handful of mixed fresh parsley and oregano, finely chopped

1 stick/110 g/4 oz butter, softened

1. Preheat the oven to 180°C/350°F/Gas Mark 4. Slice the bread into 1.5 cm/^{3}/$_4$ in rounds, cutting most of the way down but leaving the base of the loaf in one piece.

2. 2 Add the garlic and herbs to the softened butter. Stir well to combine. Spread the herby garlicky butter on one side of each round of bread. Spread any leftover butter over the top of the loaf.

3. 3 Wrap the loaf tightly in foil (if freezing, cut the loaf into portions, then wrap and freeze each portion separately). Cook in the preheated oven for 20 minutes. Let cool slightly before serving.

Baked beans

Baked beans make a filling supper, but shop-bought versions can contain lots of sugar and salt. These homemade beans are healthier and they taste so good that the grown-ups will want them too.

Makes **4** Toddler Portions

1 tbsp/15 ml olive oil

1 medium onion, finely chopped

1 garlic clove, peeled and crushed

1 cup/225 ml/8 fl oz canned crushed tomatoes or passata

1 tbsp/15 ml soy sauce

1 tbsp/15 ml Worcestershire sauce

$1/2$ tsp English mustard, or 1 tsp smooth French mustard

$1/4$ cup/50 ml/2 fl oz apple juice

freshly ground black pepper, to season

400 g/14 oz can navy (haricot) beans, drained and rinsed

1. Heat the oil in a pan. Add the onion and the garlic, and cook over low heat for 6–7 minutes, until softened but not browned.

2. Add the canned crushed tomatoes or passata, soy sauce, Worcestershire sauce, mustard, apple juice, and black pepper. Stir, then add the beans, and bring to a boil. Reduce the heat to low. Let simmer for 25 minutes, stirring from time to time, until well-cooked.

Pasta bolognese

This classic sauce is rich in iron – a nutrient that many children don't get in the recommended quantities. Serve with pasta shells (conchiglie) which hold lots of sauce.

Makes **10** Toddler Portions / Serves **4**

2–3 tbsp/30–45 ml sunflower oil

450 g/1 lb lean ground (minced) beef

1 large onion, finely chopped

400 g/14 oz can chopped tomatoes

1 tbsp/15 ml tomato puree

large pinch of dried mixed herbs

1¼ cups/300 ml/½ pint hot beef stock (made with a good
   quality stock cube)

freshly ground black pepper, to season

2 tsp/10 ml cornstarch (cornflour)

¼ cup/50 ml/2 fl oz water

freshly cooked pasta shells, to serve

1. Preheat the oven to 160°C/325°F/Gas Mark 3. Heat 1 tbsp/15 ml of the oil in an ovenproof, flameproof, lidded casserole. Brown the beef in 3 batches, turning from time to time and adding a little more oil if needed – each batch will take 3–4 minutes to brown. Set aside.

2. Heat the remaining oil in the casserole, add the onion, and cook over low heat for 6–7 minutes, until softened but not browned.

3. Add the browned mince to the softened onion together with the tomatoes, tomato puree, mixed herbs, hot stock, and black pepper. Bring to a boil, cover, and place in the preheated oven for 30 minutes or until cooked.

4. Mix the cornstarch (cornflour) with the water until smooth. Stir into the sauce, then bring to a boil. Serve over the cooked pasta.

Speedy pizza

English muffins make a superquick pizza base that's just the right size for little ones. Children will have fun spreading the tomato sauce and then sprinkling on their own cheese and oregano.

Makes **2** Toddler Portions

1 English muffin, halved

2 tbsp/30 ml smooth tomato pasta sauce (see page 58), or use a good store-bought sauce

1/4 cup/25 g/1 oz grated mozzarella or Cheddar cheese

small pinch of oregano

1. Split the muffin, and toast the outsides under the broiler (grill).

2. Spread the tomato sauce very thinly over the untoasted sides. Top with the mozzarella or Cheddar, then sprinkle the oregano over the top.

3. Broil (grill) for 2 minutes or until the cheese is bubbling. Let rest for a minute or so to cool before serving.

Lemon chicken with rice towers

A lemony marinade gives this chicken a gorgeous sweet-and-sour taste, and children will have great fun demolishing the sandcastle-like rice tower. Serve with any green vegetable for a balanced meal.

Makes **2** Toddler Portions

1 skinless chicken breast, cut into strips

1/4 cup/50 g/2 oz basmati rice

1 tbsp/15 ml olive oil

lemon marinade

juice of 1/2 lemon

1 tbsp/15 ml olive oil

1 garlic clove, peeled and crushed

1 tbsp/15 ml runny honey
   (not suitable for babies under one year)

1 tsp/5 ml soy sauce

freshly ground black pepper, to season

1. First make the marinade. Mix together the lemon juice, oil, garlic, honey, and soy sauce. Season with black pepper, then add the chicken strips and turn to coat. Let marinate in the refrigerator for 30 minutes (or a few hours if you want to make the marinade ahead of time).

2. Meanwhile, bring a small pan of water to a boil, add the rice, stir once, then let simmer for 10 minutes or until tender. Drain.

3. While the rice is cooking, heat the oil in a large skillet (frying pan). Remove the chicken from the marinade, discarding the marinade. Cook over high heat for 2–3 minutes, turning once, until completely cooked through.

4. Spoon the hot rice into 2 small pots or espresso cups. Press down, then turn out onto a plate. Arrange the cooked chicken alongside.

Mini fishcakes

These little fishcakes are fried in a mixture of butter and oil to make them extra tasty. They don't freeze well, so they are best served as a family meal, with steamed carrot sticks and green beans on the side.

Makes **10** Toddler Portions / Serves **4**

450 g/1 lb starchy (floury) potatoes, peeled and chopped into
   equal-sized chunks

generous splash of milk

knob of butter

3 tbsp/45 ml olive oil

freshly ground black pepper, to season

185 g/6^1/2 oz can salmon, or tuna in water

handful of fresh dill or parsley, finely chopped

1 tbsp/15 ml capers, chopped (optional)

flour, for coating

1. Put the potatoes into a large pan of water. Bring to a boil, then simmer for 20 minutes until soft. Drain and mash with the milk, butter, and 1 tbsp of the oil, and season with pepper. Let cool.

2. Drain the canned fish, then flake, removing any pieces of bone from the salmon, if using. Add the flaked fish to the mashed potato along with the dill or parsley and the capers, if using. Lightly mix together, then use your hands to shape the mixture into 10 small balls.

3. Sprinkle some flour over a plate. Heat the remaining oil in a large skillet (frying pan). Roll each fish ball in the flour, dust off the excess, then place in the oil. Cook for 5 minutes on each side, until golden and heated through. Press the fishcakes down slightly as they cook to make patties. Drain on paper towels before serving.

Egg strips with soupy noodles

A dish made from store-cupboard ingredients and is on the table in minutes.

Makes **1** Toddler Portion

$^1/_2$ tsp/2.5 ml low-salt vegetable bouillon powder, or $^1/_2$ low-salt vegetable stock cube

$^1/_2$ tsp/2.5 ml tomato puree

$^2/_3$ cup/150 ml/5 fl oz water

splash of mushroom ketchup or soy sauce

freshly ground black pepper, to season

40 g/1$^1/_2$ oz noodles

1 medium egg

small pinch of cayenne pepper

1 tsp/5 ml vegetable oil

1 tsp/5 ml finely chopped fresh parsley or cilantro (coriander)

1. Place the bouillon or stock cube, tomato puree, water, and mushroom ketchup or soy sauce in a small pan. Season with pepper and bring to a boil.

2. Add the noodles to the boiling stock and cook according to the packet instructions, until soft.

3. While the noodles are cooking, crack an egg into a small bowl, season with a little black pepper and the cayenne and beat to combine.

4. Heat the oil in a small skillet (frying pan). Pour in the egg mixture and swirl the pan so that it covers the base. Cook over high heat for 1 minute or until cooked. Turn or flip over the omelet and brown the other side for 30 seconds or so.

5. Transfer to a chopping board and cut into thin strips. Put the noodles into a bowl with as much of the cooking stock as liked. Top with the egg strips. Sprinkle with the parsley or cilantro (coriander).

Chicken nuggets

Here's a healthy alternative to shop-bought chicken nuggets which are usually high in salt. The chicken is cut into strips rather than chunks, so that it cooks quickly in just a little oil.

Makes **4** Toddler Portions

1 large egg

flour, for coating

freshly ground black pepper, to season

1 skinless chicken breast, cut into thin strips

1 cup /70 g/$2^{1}/_{2}$ oz fresh breadcrumbs

3 tbsp/45 ml sunflower oil

chunks of tomato and cucumber, to serve

1. Crack the egg into a small bowl, and beat. Season the flour with black pepper, then tip into a plastic food bag. Add the chicken strips and shake gently until they are well coated.

2. Place the breadcrumbs in a large, shallow bowl. Heat the oil in a large skillet (frying pan). Dip each floury nugget into the beaten egg, roll in the breadcrumbs, then transfer immediately to the pan. Cook over medium heat for 2 minutes on each side, until the coating is crispy and golden and the chicken is cooked through.

3. Drain on paper towels, then serve with chunks of tomato and cucumber.

Tasty bean spread

For a balanced quick lunch, spread this cheesy bean dip onto ricecakes or oatcakes, and offer some crunchy carrot and cucumber sticks alongside.

Makes **8** Toddler Portions / Serves **2**

400 g/14 oz can lima beans (butterbeans), drained

2 tbsp/30 ml olive oil

$^1/_2$ garlic clove, peeled and crushed

$^1/_2$ cup/50 g/2 oz grated Cheddar cheese

2 tsp/10 ml very finely chopped parsley (optional)

large pinch of paprika

1. Drain the lima beans (butterbeans) and place in a blender. Add the olive oil, garlic, Cheddar cheese, and the parsley, if using, and then season with the paprika. Blend to a thick paste.

Winter sausage hotpot

A hearty warming dish that is great to share on a cold winter's night. If you want to freeze it, you can leave out the sausages, then cook them separately when you are ready to serve.

Makes **8** Toddler Portions / Serves **4**

2 tbsp/30 ml olive oil

1 large leek, cut lengthwise and then sliced into half-moons

3 medium carrots, peeled and sliced
   (leave organic carrots unpeeled)

1 small white cabbage, shredded

2 tsp/10 ml dried mixed herbs

freshly ground black pepper, to season

8 skinless small thin sausages (chipolatas)

1 tbsp/15 ml tomato puree

5 cups/1.2 l/2 pints hot vegetable stock
   (use homemade or a good, low-salt bought stock)

1. Preheat the oven to 180°C/350°F/Gas Mark 4. Heat the oil in a flameproof, ovenproof casserole. Add the leek, carrots, and cabbage, then cook over low heat for 10 minutes or until soft and slightly browned. Stir in the mixed herbs and pepper.

2. Tuck the sausages into the vegetable mixture. Add the tomato puree to the hot stock and stir well to mix. Pour the stock over the sausage and vegetable mixture, then bring to a boil.

3. Cover the casserole and place in the preheated oven for 40 minutes. Serve with mashed potatoes and peas, or simply with crusty bread.

Hot fish triangles

A store-cupboard meal that's handy when your toddler needs feeding fast. Sardines and pilchards have soft edible bones so they are a superb non-dairy source of calcium.

Makes **2** Toddler Portions

small can of sardines or pilchards, about 150 g/5^1/$_2$ oz
   in weight

2 slices bread

^{1}/$_2$ medium tomato, cut into thin slices

freshly ground black pepper, to season

1 tsp/5 ml finely chopped fresh parsley (optional)

1. Cut down the back of the fish and take out the backbone. Discard, then mash the fish very well to crush the soft bones (take care that no hard pieces remain).

2. Toast one side of the bread. Arrange the tomato slices over the uncooked sides. Spoon the mashed fish over the top, covering the bread completely.

3. Broil (grill) for 5 minutes, or until the fish is heated through. Season with black pepper, then sprinkle with the parsley, if using. Remove the crusts, and cut the fish toasts into small triangles.

Potato cake

This version of a Spanish tortilla is great for lunch, parties, or picnics. Cut into small squares for toddlers and larger ones for grown-ups. The dish will keep for a couple of days in the refrigerator.

Makes **18** Toddler Portions / Serves **6**

2 tbsp/30 ml olive oil

675 g/1 lb 8 oz starchy (floury) potatoes, peeled, halved,
   and cut into thin half-moons

1 medium onion, halved and then cut into thin half-moons

5 large eggs

splash of milk

pinch of sea salt

freshly ground black pepper, to season

small pinch of cayenne pepper

1. Heat the oil in a large lidded skillet (frying pan). Add the potatoes and onions, and cook for 10 minutes, stirring frequently to stop them browning. Reduce the heat to very low, cover the pan, and cook for 30 minutes, stirring from time to time, until the potatoes are very soft.

2. Combine the eggs, milk, salt, pepper, and cayenne, and beat well.

3. Pour the egg mixture over the potato mixture, then stir briefly to coat. Cook, uncovered, for 20 minutes or until the egg is cooked through, gently easing the tortilla away from the sides of the pan from time to time.

4. Meanwhile, heat the broiler (grill). Place the pan with the tortilla under the broiler (grill) for 2–3 minutes to brown. Turn out and let cool for at least 10 minutes before cutting.

Spicy rice

The vegetables in this rice dish look like brilliant jewels in a pile of golden sand. Here the rice is served with chicken, but it also goes well with vegetarian or meat sausages. If freezing, leave out the chicken.

Makes **6** Toddler Portions

1 breast of chicken, skin on

2 tbsp/30 ml olive oil

juice of $1/2$ lemon

1 cup/200 g/7 oz basmati rice

1 medium onion, finely diced

1 garlic clove, peeled and crushed

1 large carrot, peeled and finely diced
   (leave organic carrots unpeeled)

1 red bell pepper, seeded and finely diced

1 medium zucchini (courgette), finely diced

3–4 flat mushrooms, finely diced

pinch of turmeric

freshly ground black pepper, to season

pinch of cayenne pepper

$1/2$ cup/50 g/2 oz frozen peas

1. Preheat the oven to 190°C/375°F/Gas Mark 5. Put the chicken onto a baking sheet, brush with 1 tsp of the oil, and pour the lemon juice over the top. Place in the oven for 20 minutes or until cooked.

2. Meanwhile, bring a small pan of water to a boil, add the rice, stir once, and simmer for 10 minutes or until tender. Drain.

3. At the same time, heat the remaining oil in a large, deep skillet (frying pan). Add the onion, garlic, carrot, bell pepper, zucchini (courgette), and mushrooms together with the turmeric, black pepper, and cayenne. Cook over medium heat, stirring occasionally, for 10 minutes or until the vegetables are soft.

4. Add the peas and cooked rice to the vegetables. Cook, stirring, for 3–4 minutes to heat through. Skin and slice chicken, and serve with the rice.

French toast

This eggy bread makes a quick, energy-giving breakfast for a cold morning – or a good snack for any time of day. Cut each slice into small oblongs and triangles to serve.

Makes **4** Toasts

1 large egg

2 tsp/10 ml milk

small pinch of crushed sea salt

freshly ground black pepper, to season

1 cm/$^1/_2$ in slices of day-old bread

knob of butter

1. Break the egg into a mixing bowl, then add the milk and the seasoning. Beat thoroughly.

2. Place the bread in a shallow dish and pour the egg mixture over the top. Turn the bread slices so that they soak up the mixture like a sponge.

3. Melt the butter in a skillet (frying pan). When it is sizzling, add the eggy bread and pour any excess mixture over the top. Cook over low-to-medium heat for about 3 minutes on each side, until the toasts are nicely browned.

Shepard's pie

A perfect family meal. Make the meaty filling ahead of time if you can and letit cool – this makes it easier to spread the warm potato over the top. Serve with garden peas.

Makes **12** Toddler Portions / Serves **4**

1 tbsp/15 ml vegetable oil

450 g/1 lb lean ground (minced) lamb

1 medium onion, finely chopped

1 large carrot, peeled and diced
   (leave organic carrots unpeeled)

2 stalks of celery, finely chopped

2 cups/450 ml/16 fl oz hot lamb or beef stock (made with low
   salt bouillon powder or a good-quality stock cube)

1 tsp/5 ml sundried tomato paste

2 tsp/10 ml cornstarch (cornflour)

1/4 cup/50 ml/2 fl oz water

Potato topping

450 g/1 lb potatoes, peeled and cut into equal-sized chunks

generous splash of milk

knob of butter

1 tbsp/15 ml olive oil

freshly ground black pepper, to season

1. Preheat the oven to 160°C/325°F/Gas Mark 3. Heat the oil in a flameproof, ovenproof, lidded casserole. Brown the lamb in 2 batches – each batch will take 3–4 minutes. Lift out with a slotted spoon, leaving the oil in the casserole. Set aside.

2. Add the onion, carrot, and celery to the oil in the casserole. Cook for 6–7 minutes, until soft.

3. Return the lamb to the casserole, together with the hot stock and tomato paste. Combine the cornstarch (cornflour) and water, and stir in. Cover and place in the oven for 30 minutes. When cooked, use a spoon to lift off any excess fat, and transfer to a baking dish. Let cool.

4. Cook the potatoes until tender (see page 92), then mash with the other topping ingredients. Spread evenly over the meat filling. Heat in the oven for 20 minutes, until piping hot.

Borshch

A Russian cabbage soup with a wonderfully sweet taste. The fun here is adding the beet (beetroot) – let your child watch as it turns the soup a vibrant purple.

Makes **20** Toddler Portions / Serves **4-6**

3 tbsp/45 ml olive or vegetable oil

1 medium onion, finely chopped

2 carrots, peeled and grated (leave organic carrots unpeeled)

squeeze of tomato puree

2 large starchy (floury) potatoes, peeled and cut into small dice

4 cups/450 g/1 lb shredded white cabbage

5 cups/1.2 l/2 pints hot vegetable or chicken stock
   (use homemade or a good, low-salt bought stock)

freshly ground black pepper, to season

1 cooked beet (beetroot), grated

sour cream or Greek yogurt, to serve

handful of fresh dill, finely chopped, to garnish

garlic bread (see page 82) or toasted pita fingers, to serve

1. Heat 1 tbsp/15 ml of the oil in a skillet (frying pan). Add the onion and carrot, and cook gently for about 10 minutes, until softened and slightly mushy but not browned. Stir in the tomato puree.

2. Heat the rest of the oil in a thick-bottomed large pan, then add the potatoes and cabbage. Cook, turning frequently, for 2–3 minutes until slightly softened, then add the onion and carrot mixture to the pan together with the hot stock and seasoning. Bring to a boil, then simmer for 15 minutes, or until the vegetables are soft.

3. Just before serving, stir in the grated beet (beetroot). Bring the soup back to a boil. To serve, add a blob of sour cream or Greek yogurt and a sprinkling of dill to each bowl, and offer garlic bread or toasted pita fingers alongside.

Mushroom carbonara

Traditional carbonara uses bacon, which is too salty for young toddlers, so this healthy version substitutes tasty mushrooms. The recipe makes one small, quick supper – increase the quantities if you want to cook it for all the family.

Makes **1** Toddler Portions

1 medium egg

1 tbsp/15 ml full-fat milk

freshly ground black pepper, to season

$1/4$ cup/25 g/1 oz dried or fresh pasta shapes

knob of butter

2–3 button mushrooms, thinly sliced

1. Break the egg into a mixing bowl, then add the milk and the seasoning. Beat thoroughly.

2. Cook the pasta in a pan of boiling water until tender but still firm to the bite. Meanwhile, heat the butter until sizzling in a small skillet (frying pan). Add the sliced mushrooms, and turn to coat. Cook for 4–5 minutes, until golden brown.

3. Drain the cooked pasta and return quickly to the pan. Pour the egg mixture over the pasta and stir over low heat until thoroughly cooked – this takes about 2 minutes. Serve the eggy pasta with the sauteed mushrooms sprinkled on top.

Cheesy stars

You need a 4-cm/1^1/$_2$-in star-shaped cutter to make 15 cheesy stars. Alternatively, use any shaped cutter, or cut the mixture into strips for cheese straws.

Makes 15 Stars

^{1}/$_3$ cup/50 g/2 oz self-rising (self-raising) flour

pinch of cayenne pepper

^{1}/$_4$ stick/25 g/1 oz butter, softened

scant 1 cup/85 g/3 oz grated Cheddar cheese

1. Preheat the oven to 200°C/400°F/Gas Mark 6. Tip all the ingredients into a large mixing bowl and use your hands to combine (you can let your children do this). The mixture will be a bit crumbly at first but it will come together if you squeeze for a minute or so.

2. Put a little extra flour on your work surface, then roll out the dough to a thickness of about 0.5 cm/^{1}/$_4$ in. Cut into stars, then re-roll any remaining dough and repeat. Place the stars on non-stick baking sheets, and cook in the preheated oven for 8–10 minutes, until lightly golden. Cool on a wire rack.

Easy-cook cookies

These cookies contain walnuts, a good source of omega-3 fatty acids and protein-rich spelt flour. They are sweetened with honey rather than sugar, which means they are not suitable for babies under one.

Makes **24** Cookies

1 1/2 cups/225 g/8 oz spelt flour

2 tsp/10 ml baking powder

1 cup/115 g/4 oz ground walnuts

1/2 cup/125 ml/4 fl oz honey, warmed

1/2 cup/125 ml/4 fl oz sunflower oil

1. Preheat the oven to 200°C/400°F/Gas Mark 6. Mix together the flour, baking powder, and walnuts.

2. Combine the honey and the oil, stirring to mix. Add to the dry ingredients, and combine.

3. Use your hands to form small balls of mixture. Place on a greased baking sheet, leaving enough space for the mixture to spread, and press each ball to flatten slightly. Cook in the preheated oven for 5 minutes, or until lightly golden. Remove with a spatula and cool on a wire rack.

Orange muffins

This simple muffin recipe uses oranges instead of the more usual banana. Orange is packed with vitamin C, and gives the cakes a deliciously moist texture.

Makes **24** Muffins

2 cups/300 g/10 oz all-purpose (plain) white flour

$1^1/_2$ tsp/7.5 ml baking powder

$^1/_4$ tsp/1.25 ml salt

$^1/_2$ cup/100 g/$3^1/_2$ oz superfine (caster) sugar

1 medium egg

1 cup/225 ml/8 fl oz milk

$^3/_4$ stick/75 g/3 oz butter, melted

5 large oranges, peeled and chopped (pips removed)

1. Preheat the oven to 200°C/400°F/Gas Mark 6. In a large bowl, mix together the flour, baking powder, salt, and sugar.

2. Crack the egg into a small bowl and beat with a fork. Combine with the milk, then stir in the melted butter. Pour the mixture into the bowl with the dry ingredients and stir briefly to combine. Take care not to overmix.

3. Stir in the chopped oranges and their juices. Put spoonfuls of the mixture into cupcake (fairy cake) cases, filling them almost to the top. Cook in the preheated oven for 18–20 minutes, or until risen and golden. Cool on a wire rack.

Everyday pancakes

Children love eating things that they have helped to make. Toddlers can help crack the eggs and pour the milk, and everyone will enjoy watching you flip the pancakes.

Makes **8** Pancakes

2 medium eggs

pinch of salt

1^1/$_4$ cups/300 ml/^{1}/$_2$ pint milk

^{3}/$_4$ cup/115 g/4 oz all-purpose (plain) flour

2 tbsp/30 ml sunflower oil

double quantity (4 tbsp/60 ml) mixed berry puree
   (see page 50), to serve

1. Preheat the oven to 120°C/250°F/Gas Mark ^{1}/$_2$.
   Put the eggs into a small mixing bowl.
   Add the salt, then pour in the milk and the
   flour. Combine with a beater or hand whisk.

2. Place the oil in a saucer or small bowl.
   Use a pastry brush or a paper towel to wipe
   a small amount of oil over the base of the
   frying pan. Pour in 3 tbsp/45 ml of the batter
   and turn the pan so that it coats the base.
   Cook for 1 minute, check that it is browned
   underneath, then flip or turn over, and cook
   the other side for a further 15–30 seconds.
   Keep warm in the oven while you cook the
   remaining pancakes in the same way.

3. To serve, spread a little fruit puree over the
   pancake, roll up, and cut into rounds for
   younger toddlers *(leave whole for older ones)*.

Hot raisin apples

Baked apples make a superb dessert for young children. These ones have a hidden core of raisins – be sure to let them cool properly before serving.

Makes **2** Apples

2 eating apples

$^1/_3$ cup/75 ml/3 fl oz water

1 tbsp/25 g/1 oz raisins

$^1/_2$ tsp/2.5 ml cinnamon

small knob of butter

plain (natural) yogurt, to serve

1. Preheat the oven to 180°C/350°F/Gas Mark 4.

2. Core the apples using a corer, then prick the skins with a fork (this stops them bursting). Place in a small ovenproof dish, and pour the water around them.

3. Loosely fill the cores with the raisins, then sprinkle a little cinnamon over each apple, and top with the butter. Cook in the preheated oven for 45 minutes, or until soft. Let cool for 10 minutes before serving with a dollop of yogurt.

Index